After Eden

Poems by

Gloria Okes Perkins

After Eden

Poems by

Gloria Okes Perkins

"Eden is that old-fashioned house we dwell in every day."

Emily Dickinson

Library of Congress Cataloging-in-Publication Data
Perkins, Gloria, 1932—
A collection of poems/Gloria Okes Perkins—1st ed.
p. cm.

"A Regal Ink Press publication"

ISBN 978-0-9842964-2-2

Designed by Stephen Cassar
Typeset in Schneidler Light (Bitstream), and Bodoni (Monotype)
Designed and Printed in the United States of America

Front and back cover photographs by Janis Geyer Shull
The House at Frankford, by Pamela Solakian
All other illustrations by Richard Shull and Janis Geyer Shull

For Dan

"If ever two were one, then surely we.
"If ever man were loved by wife, then thee."
(Anne Bradstreet, 17th century)

Acknowledgements

It is pure joy to recognize and thank the talented people who have contributed to the publication of *After Eden.* At the top of the list is Stephen Cassar, editor and designer at Regal Ink Press. I so appreciate his creative vision that brought the book into being and his inexhaustible patience with the author. I have worked with several book editors in my day, but none more skillful, steadfast, and encouraging than Stephen.

At the beginning, choosing 106 poems out of the writing of 45 years seemed a daunting task, but I accomplished it with the advice and discernment of Mary Alice Larson, a teacher of literature as well as poet, essayist, and playwright. Nothing means more to those of us who write poetry than to have it understood and appreciated. Mary Alice's "Introduction" to *After Eden* with her perceptive observations and intuitive grasp of my themes is the sort of thing a poet dreams of. I will always be grateful.

The photographs that grace this book are the work of Janis and Richard Shull, nature photographers in Mena, Arkansas. I'm thrilled with their artistry in portraying the flowers and nature scenes that communicate the heart of my poetry. Janis and I began a prayer group when we were neighbors which later became an annual writers' retreat. For twelve years our group has met, sharing our common vision and purpose as Christian writers. *After Eden* is one of the happy results.

My thanks to Jessica Rosenthal who posed for Janis in the photograph illustrating "In an Unquiet World." The poem honors my grandmother, Sue Criner, who was born on an Alabama plantation just before the Civil War. Jessica looks remarkably like Sue with her fair face and "long hair, pale as cream." It seems appropriate that she is writing on the lapboard Sue used a century or more ago.

The watercolor painting of my family home done by acclaimed California artist Pamela Solakian is one of my best-loved treasures. Pamela and I found that we shared a love of the old houses we grew up in, and her work continues to bring me joy. I am delighted to be able to show a photographic depiction of *The House at Frankford* by Pamela Solakian on the title page, even though you must imagine the glowing colors of the original work.

Many people have had a part in the poetry I write, and I want to take this opportunity to acknowledge some of them by name or group. For instance, if I had not moved to Northwest Arkansas in 1974, I might never have become a serious poet. I will always be glad for Poets Roundtable of Arkansas and the Siloam Springs Writers, especially Maggie Smith, Clara Willis, and Tom Whiteside, who kept me focused on poetry; for Dr. Lily Peter, Poet Laureate of Arkansas, who awarded me the Poet Laureate Award in the very first contest I entered; for Clovita Rice, poetry journal editor, who encouraged poets like me with her influential *Voices International;* and for Dr. John Wink and Jack Butler, poetry critics, whose insightful comments left their mark on my poems.

The Springdale Poets and Writers, an exciting association of 50 writers from Northwest Arkansas which I chaired for five years, fed my enthusiasm and spurred me on. This continued with the Christian Writers under the leadership of Lois Spoon. Today I am connected with Poets Northwest to keep the creative fires aglow and with the Siloam Springs Writers who entrust their poems to me for critique. We all learn by reading the great poets of the ages, but less-known writers have intrigued, delighted, and stirred me with their work. These poets—an incomplete list— include Mary Alice Larson, Gaylia Dalton, Patricia Brown, Elaine Soeren, Judith Walker, Barbara Evans, and Elizabeth Bartell.

After Eden is an expression of my deeply-held faith, and so I gratefully acknowledge John Glasser and Steve Barthelemy, my pastors, and Miss Carol McCormick, my Bible teacher for the past 23 years, as people who have nurtured my faith in Christ with their Scriptural teaching and the example of their lives. Dr. Ed Wheat (now deceased) and Gaye Wheat, my co-authors in the *Love-Life* books, have been a special blessing and inspiration to Dan and me.

If my parents, Guy and Irene Okes, and my Okes and Hanson grandparents could see this book, they would know they are still in my thoughts and happiest memories. Because of them and my array of aunts and uncles, I had 12 homes open to me during my growing-up years. Each contributed to the magical childhood I have translated into the poetry of this book. My cousin, Wanda Purviance, was the first (besides my mother) to collect my poems, and her encouragement, along with my Aunt Wanda Hanson's, has meant much.

No acknowledgement could be complete without thanksgiving for my strong and steady husband, Dan; for our sons, Keith and Michael, men of integrity and courage who have distinguished themselves in their chosen fields; and for our daughter-in-law, Diane, a kindred spirit whom I first met while teaching a poetry session and liked instantly.

To my precious friends—you know who you are—and our church family, you are all part of the poetry of my life. Thank you!

Gloria Okes Perkins
Springdale, Arkansas

Table of Contents

I After Eden

II Winging

III In An Unquiet World

IV In the Morning of the World

V Young on the Shore

Introduction

by Mary Alice Larson

You hold in your hands the only comprehensive collection to date of poetry by an extraordinary woman. Those who have known her as a biblical counselor or author of the *Love Life* books may have been unaware of her poetic accomplishment, much of which, in my opinion, stands equal to any in our language.

Yet there is a deep connection between her counseling and her poetry. Those who thoughtfully read Part I, "After Eden," and Part III, "In an Unquiet World" will never doubt the compassion of the author for human turmoil, bewilderment, and grief. She believes in "the God of all comfort," and every aspect of her life and work is pervaded by her profound relationship with God. She is never without a sense of the presence of her heavenly Father, in whom is her support, her peace, and her renewal. This is the explanation for the vitality of her spirit, undiminished year by year.

Gloria Sue Okes grew up in the small northeast Missouri community of Frankford (near Hannibal) during the Depression, which became Wartime. But there the world's darkness intruded lightly. Frankford was a rich, satisfying environment where most ways were the old ways still. Here, Gloria, the only little girl in two close-knit, well-esteemed families, with an abundance of grandparents, aunts, and uncles, enjoyed a freedom almost unheard-of today, freedom to roam at will, play make-believe, and breathe in the beauty of tree, flower, and farm. Central to that existence was the big white house belonging to the Okes family. A painting of the house by artist Pamela Solakian now hangs in Gloria's living room. Part IV of this book, "In the Morning of the World," is a collection of intense, brilliant scenes with their attendant emotions from that time and place. I believe a part of Gloria lives there still.

During her college years at the University of Missouri she made a life-determining commitment, and a few days after graduation, she and Everett "Dan" Perkins were married. It is impossible to doubt that a divine hand brought them together, or to overestimate the resultant blessings, not only for themselves, but also for many, many lives they have touched, as a couple, in the years since.

They have two sons, Keith and Michael, a daughter-in-law, Diane, and a surprising number of "spiritual children," as well. Their career moves have led them from St. Louis, Missouri to Rockford in Northern Illinois, then west to Fort Collins, Colorado, at the front range of the Rockies, and finally to beautiful Northwest Arkansas. It was in Rockford, in the frozen north, on her 24th birthday, that she met Jesus Christ through the pages of her Bible and made a lasting commitment to follow Him wherever He led. She notes that her physical birth and her spiritual birth both occurred during snowstorms, which perhaps accounts for the snow metaphors of her poetry.

As an Honors graduate of MU's prestigious School of Journalism, Gloria never lacked for career posts full of scope and challenge: newspaper editorships, public relations director for a large library system, and, later, after her two sons had passed childhood, as magazine editor and publications director for a international women's educational/philanthropic association. She also directed international leadership training conferences and served on the Board of Directors of the organization.

This weight of responsibilities grew in her hands, along with the work of befriending and guiding college students in their western home, until one day she and Dan and their teen-age sons knew it was time for a change. They planned a move to a quiet place, and felt themselves guided to the beauty of rural Arkansas. Here were peace and spiritual renewal. But extended inactivity? Hardly!

In Arkansas, at last, there was time for Gloria to develop the poetic potential bubbling just under the surface. The 1970's and 1980's were years of winning award after award in both regional and national poetry competitions. She also continued to employ her talents as freelance writer, critic, and editor of book manuscripts.

A natural leader, Gloria, throughout her adult life, has headed almost innumerable Bible study groups as well as formal and informal writers' associations, classes, and workshops. She is a born teacher, delighting in the creation of imaginative lessons, and has taught more people (often without pay) how to write than many who attempt this difficult task for a living. Home-schooled children, teenagers in a private high school, college students, and adults of all ages have labored with joy under her tutelage (I among them), for she has a way of enabling others to discover their own creative powers.

Arkansas opened up an even wider scope for her writing skills. Here, Gloria became acquainted with Ed Wheat, MD, a family doctor who was becoming sought after on the national stage as a notable marriage counselor. This led to their joint authorship of *Love Life for Every Married Couple* (a publishing phenomenon) and four other books whose content and counseling principles were grounded, page by page, upon the authority and wisdom of the Bible. Millions of these volumes published by Zondervan in more than thirty languages have gone throughout the world, with a resulting response from the public, and countless requests for personal help in solving marriage problems. Today, Gloria continues to receive telephone calls and letters from people all over North America, and she works by phone and e-mail with couples or individuals who are serious about saving their marriages. She and Dan frequently use their home as a meeting place to counsel and mentor younger couples, and they rejoice as they see troubled marriages transformed. They consider this one of the most important contributions they can make in today's world. It is a labor of love coming out of their more than fifty years of happiness together.

To give of the best that she has to offer is Gloria's nature; it is a trait that shines through her like sunlight. Otherwise, she is full of paradox. Her work has required her to sit at head tables and speak to large audiences, yet she dislikes the spotlight and declines speaking engagements. Her private life is kept sacred, yet dozens of friends—she continues to gather new ones—fill her days and evenings with stimulating conversation, exchanges of ideas, and fun. A woman of words and books, she has spent many an hour exulting in God's creation in the rugged out-of-doors. In contrast to her passionate affinity for old houses, story-filled heirlooms, and history, she was the first friend of my generation not only to own a computer, but to embrace it as an indispensable tool. Though steeped in the Bible and decidedly conservative in her views, she is nevertheless an up-to-the minute movie buff. While her CD collection represents eclectic tastes in music, hymns are her favorite songs, and she and Dan sing a different one together every day of the year.

For me, the greatest astonishment, yet one I thank God for, is some mysterious, unfailing power of regeneration that brings Gloria back, over and over, from health difficulties, each threatening to lay her low. Typically, her friends find that before long we are once more being welcomed at her door by an erect, glowing woman smiling at our arrival as though nothing in the world could delight her more (and I believe all visitors feel thus). Her "secret" power of renewal is no secret—it is entirely spiritual.

In this book Gloria has clarified her intentions by grouping the poems into five parts, yet the heart of each section somehow embraces all the other sections, so that the end result is greater than the sum of parts. It is as if, inside one hundred poems, we have one thousand, as the themes entwine and mutually enrich: themes of renewal, of the unsearchable ways of God, of sweetness and joy in this world, and of the complexity of the human heart.

Gloria's God is not easy. His ways are past our comprehension, she says clearly. In "Fire and the Knife" (Part III) about Abraham's climb up Mt. Moriah with Isaac , she writes of our inevitable *"journey into loss."* Snow, cold, and whiteness, which recur over and over in her work, become symbols of the unknowable aspects of the Eternal, yet these symbols shift, now appearing to represent threat, and now comfort, as in our unfinished faith we shift from fear to understanding. In "The Hunt of the Unicorn" (Part I), the whiteness of the unicorn represents not only Divine mystery, but also divine purity.

Themes of faith, love, and natural beauty are universal in Christian poetry; in Gloria's work they appear in fresh imagery, from somber to exuberant. For her, as for all true poets, the writing process is the hardest of all work—and the most exhilarating play. Part II is titled "Winging" for this feeling of thrilled uplift. In "A Prayer" to the Father of poets she asks *"...loose my mind to run among the strength of hills..."* Greatly blessed are the writers who, heavily burdened in life, can thus *"soaring take far flight..."* ("Winging").

Gloria works with all forms of poetry apparently effortlessly. She makes them look so easy! Here are some of the tightest, most difficult rhyme schemes (patterns); for some she indicates the exact name of the form. We are reminded that she has served as judge or entrant in hundreds of contests, many of which strictly prescribe a certain form. This book includes 16 examples of the sonnet, the classic 14-line form beloved through the centuries. The flowing, natural sound of iambic pentameter required for the sonnet is a staple throughout Gloria's works; I believe she often *thinks* in iambic pentameter!

Her versatility is easily demonstrated in a contrast of two poems from Section V: "Going on" and "This Ending." The latter consists of 16 lines tightly rhymed and rhythmed, and dense with the music of repeated sounds. Here are a wealth of image and color, yet soft-focused through the use of words like *"dull," "fading," "paling gray," "clouding,"* and *"worn down,"* all contributing to the idea of a year diminishing, winding down, nearly ended. Through the use of words, the overall effect is much like that of impressionism in painting.

"Going On," in contrast, has everything that can make free verse wonderful, having no formal design whatsoever, yet sharply focused as a photograph, brief and magic in its image, and clear as a bell in its intent. Free verse is the perfect choice to convey an idea of the life force itself, symbolized by the coyote, gaunt yet undaunted.

Every reader will choose favorite lines. Two of mine—out of dozens—are *"secluded room within/my spirit where the meanings grow,"* and *"to believe and wait/until apparent loss turns into gain."*

With Part V we reach a culmination of wisdom gained through new mysteries of paradox. Snow becomes a house; far from threatening, it can now be recognized as an embrace. The winter of our life is warm. Looking across years both forward and backward, we are young and old simultaneously. Renewal is eternal, along with the safety and surety of perfect peace in God. We are all *"young on the shore"* of something vast and transcendent.

It is no coincidence that the poems which begin and end this collection both picture marriage, strongest of the themes of this artist's life. Both poems, as well, are set in night time, with the implication that our sight in this world must always be "through a glass, darkly." "After Eden" is set in the cold of night and the far deeper cold of exile. The only hint of a way of redemption is through the warmth of human love.

In the final poem, what contrast! Instead of Adam's dull despair, we hear the voice of the author, speaking as herself, in calm courage and faith. "On the Long Drive North" is the narrative of a journey, the poet sitting beside her husband in the small, warm "house" of the car, protected and safe, as sturdy Dan drives through a near-blizzard toward reunion with family on the occasion of death. Here is a picture of marriage perfectly Scriptural, perfectly blest.

The unrhymed Shakespearean blank verse is handled with great mastery, as are the authentic details of the trek. Anyone who has ever driven through our country's Midlands in winter will recognize, for example, a *"gaunt white house with darkened hulk of barn."* Every word speaks true—and then come the almost unbearably beautiful, poignant concluding lines:

> *There, up ahead, a loving welcome waits . . .*
> *Light through opened doors, shining on the snow.*

Both *snow* and *light* are mighty metaphors, used together for the first time, fulfilling both the poem's promise and that of this body of work. The traveler's faith is rewarded; at the end of the journey, Love waits.

I

After Eden

"My heart cannot rest or be fully content until, rising above all gifts, and every created thing, it rests in You, O Lord."

Thomas a'Kempis,
The Imitation of Christ

After Eden

Grayed by sinning, Adam most loves the night
when cold stars penetrate the dullness
of his sight. And in the opaque dusk,
perfumed with white azalea blooms,
Adam remembers where once they freely grew,
yearns for sweet bird cries, the scents,
the dawns, the dew; white flesh luminous
in the sun, mating in Eden, all creating done;
those walks with Him who made the cool of day
for calm discourse, the hour to talk with Him . . .

When homesick for Him above all, she calls.
The strange remembered beauty of communion
with the LORD is stilled as hungers collide,
for Adam has lost his Eden, but kept his Eve
with joy and grief thus evenly implied.
When longing for the Lost Country burns
like frosty iron, he turns within
his wife's white arms, lies warmed at length
in passion's slow-evaporating light.
Grayed by sinning, Adam most loves the night.

Like An Undiscovered Star

Like an undiscovered star
this magnolia leaf has fallen
from the tree and lies in the grass
until I catch its strange loveliness
gleaming up at me.

I invent a reason for it there.
Richly brown as leather, it becomes
a supple glove dropped upon the ground
by an unknown rider who rides on.

I take it home, a trophy for my desk
and there it rests—marbled green
as Roman baths, long and curved
and pointed, graceful as a scimitar.
I study it with wonder, stroke it
with my thumb.

Weeks away from the tree
it does not crumble at my touch.
It has gained the patina of old bronze,
the texture of parchment. I stare
at its pale gold veins, its arches and whorls,
as though to find a message for my world.

But no. This leaf is separate as a star,
remote as ice cliffs in green arctic waters.
My metaphors and similes cannot ride
the distance between us or fill the silence.

For now I see
humankind long fallen from the tree
and this lovely silent leaf
observing me.

By Design

for Kathaleen

Before such things as stars were made to flame
throughout the endless, frozen realms of space,
then, even then, the mystery of grace,
though only eons later known by Name,
both chose and wove the pattern sure to tame
this one, unruly, fraying as worn lace,
resistant, tangled, hurting, lost, this face
a mask, a child's, this life devoid of aim.

Now Love would speak to her: "Child, do not fear,
for change is motion working out My will;
I plan it all by intricate design.
Beyond your turning trials, year by year,
a spiral turning, not the grim treadmill,
I see a lovely woman, wholly Mine."

The Hunt of the Unicorn

after *The Unicorn Tapestries*
"The unicorn who is hunted...is the Christ."
Romare Bearden

I

Out of the unformed darkness comes the beast
with tender tread, to prick my small-child state
until, in longing lost, I turn to feast
most richly at Imagination's plate.
Yet in the bright-twined weavings of this art,
I strangely lose the scent and inner sight
of that which first aroused my sleeping heart
to seek the nameless source of sweet delight.
The Unicorn has left his mark on me:
a tiny wound, it throbs as though heart-deep
in earth-hushed summer dawns, or majesty
of sunset fires, or in my dream-flushed sleep.
  Full-grown from child to woman, now I find
  the search goes on in reaches of my mind.

II

I circle Truth as though it were a glass,
possessed and filled by jealous gods who hoard
the best of wisdom and refuse to pass
their nectar on in private thimbles poured.
I handle Truth as though it might soon crack,
as brittle glass unsafe in heat and cold,
and I, the clumsy housemaid with no knack
for dusting treasure costlier than gold.
Yet Truth rings diamond-hard and harder still:
unchanging clarity expressed by light
applied in countless colors at the will
of him who freely gave the blind man sight.
  Truth radiates its force, a fiery sun
  whose rays can heal—or blind the careless one.

(cont.)

III

While following the Unicorn, I've turned
into an old-grown tangled thicket, dense,
impassable with cluttered theories learned
in homage to man's own intelligence.
This path through territories of the mind
leads nowhere. Up ahead, the Unicorn
has paused beside a fountain, unconfined,
with tranquil blue-deep eyes and kingly horn.
The hunt's resigned—impossible to seize
and harness him, a trophy for my pride.
I see that you, Lord Truth, choose whom you please
to walk behind or cling to your great side.
    Now I, a wanderer in Christendom,
    am found at last, for—hunting me—you come!

The God Who Calls

The blasting heat of the desert
melts itself
when the bush begins to burn.
Sandy wind silences
and bare rock must turn
to see the sight—
the God of Light
covering one lone shepherd
with His call.

Is there room for argument
so encircled there
by Holy Sound?
Naked feet curl away,
say no to Holy Ground,
with maybes, buts, "who me's?"—
incompetent pleas,
yet God will not turn off
His Call.

He floods the mount with promises
searching the dark,
igniting inability
with Eternal spark:
Certainly I will be with you.
My Name is I AM
through all that waits ahead.

The shepherd is called.
Pharaoh shivers in his sleep
while slave cries still rise
to the God of Abraham,
tears seeping from unseeing eyes.
Great transitions once begun
must move until all is done
according to
the One Who Calls.

A Small Wild Cherry

In the mountains of Dalmatia
a small wild cherry grows
tart black
coruscating faintly in a Slavic sun
tempting none.

Natives know better
than to mouth it,
marasca is its name.
Call it bitter
till time and artistry
combine
a cordial to distill

Red red
sweet sweet
and the maraschino cherry
becomes the very peak
of piled up sweets
in Wichita and Coffeyville.

Naomi of Bibleland,
deprived of all she loved,
said, *Mara* is my name,
call me bitter.
But to Bethlehem she came
at the beginning of harvest.
The sweet psalmist of Israel,
he would be the harvest.

Bitter to sweet
God distills
in His plan diurnal.
Life's but a small wild cherry
in the mountains of Eternal.

How Much Do You Know?

A Ballade after *Job 38-42*

Have you ever commanded the dawn
 Or given orders to the sea?
Have you gently instructed a fawn
 Or designed the perfect oak tree?
 Have you danced with a fat bumblebee
Or tamed for the riding, a roe?
 Have you talked with a young chickadee?
How much, little one, do you know?

Have you heard the dew-song of the lawn,
 The hum of the climbing sweet pea?
Have you flown with the trumpeter swan
 Or geese in their arrow-shaped vee?
 Have you found the east wind, set it free,
Or hoarded in secret the snow?
 Have you formed winter grass for the lea?
How much, little one, do you know?

Have you seen where the unicorn spawn
 Or sought out the sharks' company?
Have you questioned the freshwater prawn
 Or psychoanalyzed the flea?
 Have you memorized every decree?
Is there any place left to go?
 Have you mastered your life's mystery?
How much, little one, do you know?

Envoi
Then the Lord who esteems honesty
 Asks the question most apropos:
Since wisdom comes through knowledge of Me,
 How much, little one, do you know?

Sunday at Black Canyon

Colorado's Black Canyon of the Gunnison

I gaze
down from sunlit rim
to deep-scarred canyon walls stained black,
and I know
that even there in lonely shaft,
place of desolation stark,
God dwells.

A Greater Than Mere Time Is Here

Time roars around the corners like a wind
with ruthless voice or dreary, ragged cry;
yet Time can masquerade as quiet friend
with speech as soft as mama's lullaby.
Time comes, an austere healer to the grieved,
or will not come at all when needed most;
in that, of course, we humans are deceived,
for Time is not our servant, but our host.
And yet a Greater than mere Time is here,
Who orders suns and shapes men's minds to see
in patterns—day to week and month to year—
that we might co-exist with mystery;
  Who promises that in some quick-drawn breath
  will come the end of Time, the death of Death.

Alone in Rome

"Alone in Rome. Why, Rome is lonely too." *
Another poet penned those brooding words,
betrayed by hopes that centered on a place,
for men of earth expect a new locale
will solve their puzzles, or apply the salve
of comfort to their self-inflicted wounds,
or introduce new joy upon the stage
now dimming with the boredom of their play.
A falsehood, this attaching dreams to land,
though travel agents thrive on such bright lies.

No need to take a flight to Greece or Rome.
The Love Boat sails without a guarantee.
So face the winter fact of solitude,
I tell myself, and chill before the truth.
Of all the world's hard anguish, I have found
that loneliness evokes the dullest pain,
a weary monotone of empty ache
the heart can register and then beat on
as though to be deprived were nothing much.
It's strange how much the heart can live without.

And yet I know beyond astonishment
that hope commends itself. There's something more
to balance out the minus of my need.
It comes like thunder's promise of cool rain
when all the world is shriveling and sere;
it speaks from the secluded room within
my spirit where the meanings grow and flower;
it rings with truth from everlasting rock
that one can surely build a life upon,
and guarantees that I am not alone.

* from Ralph W. Emerson's *"In Rome"*

Hymn for February

"Let everything that hath breath praise the Lord."
Psalm 150:6

The sodden yard replete with melted snow
seems faintly green today
as though a better thing shone through
the leaves dun-colored by the wear of feet
and weather beating down.

A hymn of hope, this seems
to my uncertain heart, and yet, eye upon
the neutral sky, I ask:
Will hope someday fail to green
and I succumb to weathering,
silent under snow?

A blue jay, sharp and crested,
commands the sodden yard as though a king
at banqueting, and struts his answer: Never!
But He who calls each star by private name,
who sees blue feathers fall—He knows.

Walking on Water

after Tintoretto's *Christ at the Sea of Galilee*

He calls across the water, calls to me,
trapped in this boat whose battered timbers groan
under the lash of winds and raging sea,
while helpless sailors grip the planks and moan.
He summons me above the eerie cry
of stricken men in chaos born of fear,
holds out His hand to me to fortify
the sudden rush of faith that brings me here:
Out of the boat on waves solid as glass,
an obsidian sea I walk upon,
like shifting mountains that must let me pass,
the light of Him before me as the dawn.
   When you are trapped by fear, adrift from land,
   then look toward shore—Christ stretches forth His hand.

The Day Whose Gift Is Rain

for Wanda

Rain snaps the sun-dried, curling leaves
and shreds the faded rose called Peace
like pinkish-gold confetti
on the cobbled walk where yesterday
I paced a rhythm out of rage.

That anger that holds longing at its core
had taken root in shimmering air,
had fed on heat, shooting forth
until its tall-grown blossoms, bronzed
by white-gold stabs of sun,
overcame the moss-cool stones
and swallowed all gentility.

But now—the gift of rain.

I thought perhaps a pelting hail,
so well-deserved, would come
to clear the ground, but rain instead,
like steady reason, does the cleansing
with its drenching—separates my longing
from the hard seed-coat of anger,
leaves it bare and gentled as with goodness
from a source beyond myself.

This gift of rain brings ambience
of grace I've yet to taste, and promises
a day when grace will be the very air I breathe
and my established home.

For now—the gift of rain—it is enough.

Message for a Sunny Day

from Peter, Paul, and Joshua

A cat dozes there in the sun,
quietly purring,
but no less dangerous
in contentment.

Its claws never sleep, but pause
for a ready prey:
the soft unprotected breast,
a flash! and blood comes,
drawn by the waiting foe.

What secret armor shall I wear
in tranquility when, unsuspected,
the claws of my enemy streak,
and I am wounded?

Beware of contentment in the sun,
a soft passive ease. Far better
the surging heart that drives ahead.

Seeking is safer than surfeit
and open conflict
defeats the deceit of him
who is the enemy of my soul.

All my days must be spent
as a soldier armed for victory,
never trusting in the safety
of a sunny day.

Opened Door

The fluffed-up clouds in iris evening sky
so whet my spirit's shrinking appetite,
that, suddenly refreshed, I find delight
in tinted fresh peach sherbet clouds piled high
on plate of crystal blue no wealth could buy.
I taste in full the glories of the sight
but cannot store it up for some dark night
and must release its wonder with a sigh.

Another time, I pray, the Lord will bless
with passing beauty colored by His art
that satisfies, yet leaves a taste for more;
this tingling sense of His vast loveliness,
it pierces to the root of earthbound heart,
this hint of Heaven seen through opened door.

The Double Rainbow

at Eagle's Loft, Pagosa Springs, Colorado

We see it in the eastern sky
late in the afternoon as mountains turn
intensely blue against the golden burn
of the round setting sun.

A thunderstorm has rumbled by
with winds that shook the aspen as they churned
the clouds to foamy gray and left leaves ferned
with raindrops. Reflection

Paints concentric colored bands. But *why*
the second rainbow—violet, indigo, blue,
green, yellow, orange, red—in arches artist-true?
His love is the reason.

From Him, this dazzling, heavenly surprise!
Unsought, His double blessing fills our eyes.

Survivors
In the High Country

Little violet pasque flowers (anemones) bloom at Easter in the High Country where it is still winter, and somehow they survive. Life may call on us to be "windflowers" too.

This could be land
of furred white bears,
blue seal waters
deep as world's end,
icebergs groaning.

A pierce of sun
harpoons the moment,
laughter freezes on my breath.

For here, the endless
arcing, bone-white
ground, stone-white
hills where wind skims
joy, skins soul,
and what's left shudders.

The High Country smiles
harshly, given to triumph.
Yet I find pasque flowers,
bewildered, windshaken,
holding on.

In Winter's Hold

Rough spring, I know no reason for this cold
that browns the blossoms on the young green stems
and mourns with rising winds, like requiems,
these seeded hopes grown prematurely old.
As tiresome anecdotes too often told,
so endless sleet has nagged the maple limbs
that should by now be laced with leafy hems—
all life seems impotent in winter's hold.

And yet the birds still sing with gallantry,
their voices lifted even in cold rain,
as though a choir director stood above
bedraggled earth to call forth melody,
to testify that out of ancient pain
one purpose through the ages rules in love.

Windswept

West Wind, High Wind, White Wind,
sweep clean the winter scene,
singing as you sweep.

High Wind, I watch you brush
dappled foothills till the pines
bristle in blue-green clusters.

White Wind, I see you polish
the silver lake as waves surge
sparkling past old ice.

West Wind, I hear you chant
a wild tune as you work
while pliant willows clap and bow.

High West Wind, you sweep clean,
no corner escapes, clutter is undone,
all that could be shaken is gone.

White Wind, you sting my spirit,
you shock me alive
with battering freshness.

II

Winging

"There is a Divine Center, an orientation in God, a center where you live with Him and out of which you see all of life through new and radiant vision."

Thomas R. Kelly,
A Testament of Devotion

Winging

The comfort of deep thunder in the sky,
the spray of water drops from fresh-blown rain,
the kindly gray of clouds, the gentle cry
of doves, the scent of purple grapes near by,
and beyond the long day's loss I wing again.

Winging comes when least we know
of fragile beating past resistant air,
pulled down by nagging weights of care,
hope fleeting, our eagle sight brought low.
A regimented din of drums,
yet winging comes.

Some living things fly passively, take speed
by riding free on strong updrafts of air:
the downy thistle, delicate milkweed,
those whirling capsules bearing maple seed,
the spider on a wisp from homespun lair.

But let me turn on wings that lift
by the spirit's power, and soaring take far flight
through the regions of the night
to find the sunrise hour spread out as gift
for those who yearn
to know the lift and skyward turn.

dark against the snow
young wild turkeys by the road
sudden rush of wings

The Poet's Way

"Friday I tasted life. It was a vast morsel."
in a letter from Emily Dickinson

Bring me the sunset in a cup, she said.
She called for life, who did not choose to go
beyond her garden gate for secret dread,
and yet she owned the world in cameo.
She tasted life, then shared it in a spread
of tangy verse—a feast, an overflow.
This poet penned her words with quick, deft skill
as one impatient, hungry, thirsting still.

Another taste she whetted with her rhyme
for worlds beyond, as positive as sound,
invisible like music with the chime
of secret suns and summers long renowned,
yet seldom heard this side of Heaven's time,
so muffled by the weight of tomb and mound.
She deigned to ride Death's shoulders on her way
and raced into the East ahead of Day.

This way creative minds mix mystery
with native wonders, tangible and small—
connect a fly's buzz with eternity
or view a bumblebee and see the Fall.
For poets fit the facts in symmetry
and find in the finite the dazzling All.
The miracle of metaphor gives birth
to lyric glory rooted in the earth.

Writer's Problem

a Pantoum

Ideas fly in like flocks of colored birds
And settle on the fresh green field awhile.
I try to capture them in nets of words
Before they leave for their enchanted isle.

They settle on the fresh green field awhile,
Their brilliant plumage shimmering in light,
Before they leave for their enchanted isle—
Ideas like feathered things in startled flight.

Their brilliant plumage shimmering in light,
They leave behind the sense of wonder lost;
Ideas like feathered things in startled flight,
And afterward on barren field, the frost.

They leave behind the sense of wonder lost.
I tried to capture them in nets of words,
But afterward on barren field, the frost.
Ideas fly off like flocks of restless birds.

A Prayer

Arrange my room until this crystal flask
fits well upon the table with the bowl
of springing, rampant tulips—so I ask
for order at the center of my soul.

Seed all my acreage with one clear goal,
implanted deep to flourish in the sun.
To make of measured time a fertile whole,
combine my several longings into one.

Fling wide my space and loose my mind to run
among the strength of hills, inviolate.
Grant form to what I find there. Once it's done,
let steady form and fiery substance mate.

Father of poets, I plead for even more:
A universal voice, an open door.

On Bur Oak Road

Dark moons,
these months now melted from my life.

The night-touched water
reflects nothing at all.

But there, beneath the surface,
something moves.

Wine Spill

Wine spill of claret,
          pink champagne,
burgundy, sherry,
          violet stain.

In heated moment
          the goblet fills,
and still wine flashing
          over-spills!

Winepress of words,
          the grape of desire,
memory's flush,
          the spirit's fire.

To taste of this wine,
          to pour it at will
is the poet's reward.
          Come, wine spill!

Maker of Worlds

With words no less than oils or chiseled stone,
With verse no less than skilled photography,
With crafted lines no less than stitchery,
I bring to being flower, flesh, and bone.
For artists can assume a lordly tone,
Creating and disposing by decree;
Just so, I raise the rod of poetry
To form the worlds I name and call my own.

A poem, small, complete, and self-possessed,
By its coherence brings an ordered view
And gathers up the shards of shattered days.
When I make worlds, the act is doubly blessed:
While I shape lucid figures of the true,
Sweet clarity unites my complex ways.

Rose of Sharon

I picked this blossom in Arkansas to study on the way to North Carolina. I wanted to describe it without the easy music of rhyme or the looseness of free verse, so I chose tetrameter, using each of the 16 metric feet of poetry at least once.

I pluck a blossom from the bush.
Petals white as a china cup,
five in all, they curve together
at the base where I see a starfish,
miniature, yet perfect in its shape.
Spring green it is. There from its heart
eruptions of creamy plumes
come forth as a floral surprise.
Gorgeous as amethysts are marks
of crimson on each pale petal.
Alluringly like a glass for elves,
iridescent goblet bearing dew,
this blossom is adaptable,
a sumptuous, sensuous world
for ants. And many such flowers
clothe the lovely Althea bush.

Like Moss I Thrive

I thank my God for quiet skies,
  the fields green after rain,
  white daisies in the lane,
All gentle sights that soothe my eyes
  and calm my hectic heart;
  like moss I thrive apart
While stillness heals a hundred sighs.

Sanctuary

walled garden
quiet chapel
a house
secluded—
    sanctuaries

one bird sings
in the rain
  hidden
by pink-feathered
mimosa blossoms

the love
of sanctuary
drowns me in gentle depths
    wishing it so

In Perspective

The dust of August grays the green elm leaves
already thinned like parchment by the sun;
the falling, then the fire for these poor sheaves
that cling to life while summer ends its run.
From this bare fact of seasonal distress—
of growing things that please the eye in June,
then dwindle into dull unloveliness—
I read a meaning traced as from a rune:
How on a star-lit night, seen from below,
from hammock gently drifting with the air,
this tree becomes, for love of soft moon glow,
a vase of creamy blossoms, rich and rare,
  Which shows me, if I'd make my world anew,
  that transformation comes with change of view.

Fountains

A brook, there was, that failed. The dearth spread wide
on sun-cracked ground where lilies once had grown
along a green and lovely waterside.

Gone too, the sound of water over stone,
swift singing like the rush of country hymns;
instead, the rocks are heaped up there alone.

A wild thing, subject to its natural whims,
this brook ran dry for want of steady rain,
while fountains fairly overflowed their rims.

For fountains are connected to the Main,
by outside power their supply is driven,
and discipline of pipes brings them their gain:

In drought-time all they need is freely given.
When brooks do fail, fine fountains rise to Heaven.

Seascape

I'll paint the sea gulls wheeling free,
the conch shells tinted peach,
awash on white sand beach,
Sketch patterns made by surging sea
where earth and water meet,
embrace and then retreat—
These beauties drawn from memory.

Or when at night my dreams take shape,
the sea is there, is there,
and I, without a care,
Partaking of the summer's grape,
can wade among the waves,
explore small ocean caves,
And ride the dolphins round the Cape.

Too long it's been since I could view
the sapphire sweep of sea,
the beaches lost to me;
For now I taste the herb of rue
and paint my seascapes bright,
with moments of delight
When dreaming seashores I once knew.

Paris on a Rainy Day

After Caillebotte's *Paris, A Rainy Day*
(Intersection of Rue d'Turin and Rue d'Moscou), 1877

The Paris rain falls fine and gray
on new-laid cobblestone,
for Caillebotte observed the way
the Paris rain fell fine and gray,
and saved, in part, this fragile day
for viewers yet unknown.
The Paris rain falls fine and gray
on new-laid cobblestone.

His brush on canvas, tone by tone,
has made the day sublime.
That passing hour becomes our own
through oils on canvas, tone by tone,
the dark-clad people deftly shown,
preserved within their time.
His brush on canvas, tone by tone,
has made the day sublime.

Sedately strolling in the rain,
these people still do live,
Parisians, elegant, urbane,
sedately strolling in the rain,
forever dwelling in Cockaigne—
life the artist can give.
Sedately strolling in the rain,
these people still do live.

I wonder if the painter knew
his vaster sense of Place,
informing, could transmute our view;
I wonder if the artist knew
that what he painted would imbue
our own brief hour with grace.
I wonder if the painter knew
His vaster sense of Place.

Tapestry

I see the light white pattering of snow
fall whisper-soft upon this small brown pool
where golden-speckled carp move with the flow
of waters cupped within its rocky cool.

And where last year's long grass leans pale as straw,
I find a clump of violets pushed through,
their blue beginnings watered by a thaw,
now by this snowfall delicate as dew.

The browns and mottled gold and snowflake white
shift into patterns like the complex weaves
of some en-towered princess who, by night,
must spin in beauty while she softly grieves.

But now and then the tender blue appears—
a motif of the hope of patient years.

When Late the Blooming

The starry daffodils this year bloomed late,
the hyacinth and dogwood were delayed,
and grass deferred its emerald turning long
as though all loveliness must hesitate
and fundamental hope begin to fade
when spring is silenced in its ancient song.

To watch with eagerness could not be wrong,
to wish for sun in place of chilly shade
or gentle warmth instead of icy rain,
and yet our highest goals may be betrayed
by our reluctance to believe and wait
until apparent loss turns into gain.
God's promise rested on will long sustain
and steadfast faith give cause to celebrate.

The Teacher

A teacher is . . .

a pebble dropped into a still pool

a bulldozer clearing space
for planting seed

intermittent rain fresh and cool

when all the magic works, a shaft
of light piercing the clouded day

an organizer of the universe

a stonemason chipping away

and at the heart of definition—
one who cares.

III

In An Unquiet World

"The Lord is King,
be the people never so impatient,
be the earth never so unquiet."
Psalm 99:1
The Book of Common Prayer

In An Unquiet World

"Come away, O human child
To the waters and the wild...
For the world's more full of weeping than you can understand."
William Butler Yeats

A cobweb of innocence shields the young girl
writing in her journal of lawful dreams.
While the plantation soaks in sweeps of rain,
she writes by candlelight on her lapboard
of yellow wood taken from virgin pine.

The elven folk might envy her fair face,
hair long and pale as cream, her clean profile
caught by candle shine in the shadowy room.
The sprite at eight, the Celtic queen at eighteen,
the calm, contained lady of eighty years
facing the fission of her world—they all are here.

Her quilt of poppies intricately linked
will survive war, neglect, the effects of time,
and life's spontaneous breaking into parts.
Even now a sibyl might sense the steel within
her gentle presence, the level gaze that one day
may replace this luminous light in her wide, gray eyes.

The creek roars with the rain that rushes its banks.
A sudden draft creaks the door half open.
The candle flame flutters while she writes on.

The Unloved Child

The unloved child bears
  a special wound:
  his heart is torn out daily.
Yet night by night he stuffs it in
  and tries again.
The wound will never heal
  where no love is.

Alone

In mountains
ridged like bones
as old as time's toll of kingdoms,
a little girl is lost.

She clutches at leaves,
clings to a sun-warmed stone,
later, calls to the amber moon
and the fretted stars, alone

Till men come with their boots
striking the ground,
their rough, glad speech—
"Found! She's found!"

The summits ring,
from the ridges, cheers,
while the clouds dissolve
in rosy light.

But the child cries softly
against a stiff woolen sleeve,
and the thud of one heart
signifies eons of need.

An Island in the Ocean

Aloneness
or loneliness,
which shall it be?
What name should I give
to the mystery
  of myself?

The sky seems
crowded with stars,
yet each, apart,
throbs into the night
as the single heart
  beats, alone.

An island
in the ocean,
this pictures me,
with view of other
islands in the sea,
  yet lonely.

Could God's hand
merge star with star,
the islands too,
if I but asked it,
then what would I do
  with this self?

(cont.)

I would stay
aloof from all,
if I must choose,
while gaining solace,
to finally lose
    my being.

Aloneness—
I accept it
with whatever pain,
grief or singing joy
my path may contain.
    Here, I begin.

Beauty's Beast

Beauty:

I dreamed a tawny cougar came to me,
came right up to my door and wanted in,
as though, beneath the surface, we were kin,
and he could claim my hospitality.
An untamed jungle cat! What mystery
brought him into my world, the world of men?
He bounded for my throat—I thought—but then
I found myself embraced most tenderly.

Wisdom:

Awaken from your dream and see the beast,
fearful of cage, cautious of love's demands,
aloof and dangerous, yet poised to feast
on honey from your open, gentle hands.
And, if you dare, wait till his pain has ceased,
until, transformed, the young prince understands.

Eros Arriving

"And love shall be more than a guest."
C. Day-Lewis

Love paces through the empty halls by night
And calls awake the tardy morning star;
Love steals into the inner room as light,
And lodges there where deepest meanings are.

Love sometimes enters openly like fate,
Or—unadmitted—crashes at the gate.

Parting

The space that night between them
grew great with sky,
wide with white, uncertain stars.

He leaned away—
or was it she who turned?
The trees took on stern shapes
as his familiar face and trusted eyes
moved into shadows,
beyond surmise.

The clang of iron
sounded in his silence.
Her words attempted entrance,
small as petals falling in the dark,
and were refused.

After the parting of mind and heart,
the silence called to her by name
and she walked away
into the distance between them.

I Will Have Coolness

for Jadwiga

Make all my flowers white—
Madonna lilies, great hydrangeas,
roses, rhododendrons,
petunias, tall delphiniums,
closed-lip snapdragons—all white
as Chinese silk
or milk,
or a remote summer moon
suspended high in frozen space.
My garden will be entirely walled
with one small arched gate.
Let the leaves
be silvered by the breeze,
and let there be
Russian olive trees.

Carve the garden bench
of marble without a hint
of green, put it by the stream,
and let the water
there be seen to foam silver
over rock as white as virgin snow,
as white as bridal lace
from an unused trousseau.
Place one sculpture here:
The Snow Maiden.
Allow a single frozen tear.
Let the statue show the sheen of ice,
for I will have coolness
in my garden, in my life.

Anne, Why Do You Weep?

Anne, why do you weep
these tears, these jewel
drops stored, hid for years
in the vault of your mind?

Why now, so late, when
the sun has pierced
its closing shafts into
the afternoon and struck
the swallows turning home
with rosy wounds?

I could not sooner
for I must preserve a clear
still surface, glass uncracked,
cool as ice unmelted, never melted.
This my only safety, proof of strength.

And now it does not matter—
let the glass shiver into
thousandth particle, let the
tears salt my house, my world
in raging flood.

For he has gone to one
who often cries
in pretty confusion
while I—
I have come to the end
of all I was.
Now, at sundown.

While the Hostess Handles Fine China With Great Care

She places china in the suds to soak,
the steamy warmth before her eyes like smoke,
and while she fingers what she cannot see,
her mind prefers to play with mystery—
how faces drawn by curling candlelight
take on a different cast as though the night
had called forth secret passions well-concealed
until by shifting shadows half-revealed.

Thus, idly, she begins to analyze,
to view each dinner guest with probing eyes.
So merciless her musings with each swish
of fragile cup and rinse of dainty dish,
forgetting how the heart may also break,
for more than costly china is at stake.

Marsha's Eulogy

Verd Z. Pinker loved his wife,
told them he did when they inked
his fingers, locked him in the cell.

"Marsha treated me good fer years,
she were one grand woman,"
he insisted to the shadows
while the cold seeped in,
blued his face, chilled his tears.

"It weren't nobody's fault
when she died," he sighed.
"I had just finished milkin', you see,
and come in the door to find
our no-count neighbor pesterin' her
like he done before. I told him to git
or I'd tend to him, but Marsha,
feelin' pity—she were a Christian woman,
you see—moved in front of me to save
his face. Well, she fell
against the stone fireplace....Fine
Arkansas stone that hearth were.
I fixed it up right for her, and I knowed
she were proud whether she said thanks
out loud, for she showed it off
to the extension club, and it were told to me...

(cont.)

"Tonight she wore her new pink dress,
looked purty as a wildflower,
big-eyed as a deer...I think
it'd distress her some to see me locked
in here. Why, she always did love *everbody.*
Even that black-haired fiddler
I caught a'kissin' her at the dance
last year...even that red-lipped, fancy pants,
no-count neighbor....

"It weren't nobody's fault," he told
the shadows, the cold, and shuddered,
silent.

Tanglewood

Thalia's Dream

The waterbed receives her, and she dreams
of some old forest and her going there,
brave as a child who does not know about
the blackbeard sleeping in a hidden cave,
resting on leaves inside the night-dark room
where water trickles down to hollowed stone.

She only knows this wood seems ominous.
Passing under peach trees growing wild,
she enters a tangled place she cannot name.

The path hides itself; greenness crowds her way.
She feels the forest with eyes closed—the bark
of hickory, the scrape of rough elm limbs,
the nibbling gnats that hum while berry thorns
tear at her skin until the blood stands forth.
She tastes it on her tongue as beaded salt.

At center point the scene blurs, then dissolves.
As tangled forest melts away, she turns
to burrow into darkness without stars.

When she awakes, the stone within her heart,
compressed of ancient guilt and silent years,
is pitched down to the bottom of that well
convenient for troubled minds that dream,
and she fries eggs for breakfast just as though
tangles could be dispelled by pale sunshine.

She later writes a poem which begins:
On which green yesterday did I taste
peaches plucked from the forbidden tree?

At the Summit

Massanutten, Virginia

Mountains
massing around me,
fold upon fold of shade and light,
trees close-ranked,
an alert green population
waiting marching orders while
I doze.

Frontier Woman

Melly South migrated over mountains to western Pennsylvania,
wearing leather moccasins tied round her ankles,
stuffed with leaves for warmth, but wet as water
half the time. She and hers were called frontiersmen,
sometimes starving ragtags, always tough as thistles,
and they founded family fortunes down the line.

Melly's husband, Isaac, gave her two sons, Dan and Jake,
and a little girl, Eliza, who early died of croup
in spite of the remedy: roasted onion juice. They migrated
in the month of April, sowed potatoes, squash, and corn;
in the meantime lived on bear meat, and built
their small rough home: walls of logs, bare earth
for floor, windowless, dark, a heavy door,
and a ring of ugly tree stumps round the yard.

Not for beauty, but for safety, Melly, boys, and husband
lived. The dread Shawnee haunted all their dreams.
For this, their gravest peril, Isaac kept his long gun
always near. Whenever natural hazards threatened
grim disaster, Melly faced them calmly,
without a single tear.

Melly's hair was long and curling, her sweet face
pert, if pale, and in her linsey petticoat
she looked as appetizing as a brown thrush to its male.
A lively girl, she loved to dance, and Isaac loved
to watch her. The rude crude fort had
two quick fiddlers and she was all the favorite—
skirts a-swinging, long curls floating, dimples showing…

(cont.)

Sudden terror! Invading Shawnee warriors with painted faces,
hideous howls, after silently destroying all the guards.
The tricked frontiersmen could never reach their weapons,
no, not in time. The dancers stopped forever.

Isaac met a tomahawk, Dan was half-scalped, left for dead,
survived a wounding in his head, while younger brother Jake
hid throughout the horror in an almost empty water barrel.
Both boys grew to toughened manhood, but, orphaned,
grew alone, for Melly's fate is shadowed. She had known
the risk of capture, the knife-edge poised above
the changing seasons of her labors mixed with love.

While whirling in the dance she saw the braves
come through the door. In that instant
all things changed, could never be as before.
One lean savage, haughty of mien, a chief with burning eyes,
grabbed her off the floor. She clawed his face
till the blood ran down, mingled with the warpaint.
She fought in desperation, fought for more than life.
But he took her, screaming, with him to become a slave—
or his wife.

That is all we know of brave young Melly,
(when last seen, still alive!)
that strong frontier woman of Seventeen-Sixty-Five.

Gray Remembrance

I saw the spider in the corner, meek
and unobtrusive, spinning out her silk.

Self-
contained,
she
only
asked
for
space,

this territory which I never used and she,
so small and purposeful, required.

"Look there," my neighbor said, "A black widow,
most likely, or it could be a brown recluse!"
Virtuously, he smashed it with his shoe.

I walked away silent, my chest on fire.
The spider did not demand my pity—
It was gone as if it had never been.

But the gray web glistening in hard sunlight

hung
there
long,

a tattered remembrance of life
obliterated by virtuous men.

The Hunter

The hunter trapped for muskrat, fox, and mink,
and breakfasted on rabbit, crisp and brown;
he hunted game the way men like to think
they could if free to stalk the deer's home ground.
His eyes pierced keen as blades, their reach was long;
relentlessly he tracked his prey with gun
held ready for the kill, his forearms strong,
his light quick feet untiring on the run.
But here he rests as still as stone—or clay,
his sunken frame encased in suit and tie.
The hunter has himself become the prey,
tracked down by ruthless Time to age and die:
  Laid out on satin pillows frilled and white,
  now caught in all the trappings of long night.

They Think Her Old

The lines
of age cut deep,
but deeper yet, the pleasant scorn
of those who own few years and sleep
with ease of babe
new-born.

They think
of her as old
and do not know her springing heart
that, young and hungry, yearns to hold
to life, and aches...
apart.

Gilda

(Rita Hayworth, who played
the unforgettable *Gilda*,
died of Alzheimer's at age 68.)

Rita must be

Forever Gilda
long after the
amber eyes dull,
the red-gold mane

Is sheared,
the husky voice,
cracked by time,
forgets the words:

*"Put the blame on
Mame, boys..."*
What comes next
will never be known

Nor will the Glenn Ford
of this merciless day
relent his prognosis
and shower hope and love

On the innocent—
lovely, innocent Gilda,
now caged by age
and mishap of the genes.

Poor Rita,
I wish you could be
Gilda again,
Gilda unloosed

For all of us.

The Sand Builder's Story

After *Matthew* 7:26-27

Because I know the ancient urge to build
some structure that will be entirely mine,
(as yet, my fond ambitions unfulfilled)
I diagram a masterful design.
I search below the beach's crest for sand
precisely damp enough where waves retreat.
Ten hours between the tides that claim the land
to make my fortress by the sea complete.

I press and mold the sand until it cakes,
I form the mound and buttresses and towers,
I dig a moat with well-arched bridge; it takes
the better part of my allotted hours.
I wield a putty knife to shape the stairs,
and terrace with my store of white driftwood.
I carve and sculpt and stop to make repairs,
I work as hard as any builder could.

For when the sun has spilled into the sea
I gaze with pleasure on my craft of hand,
this structure shaped with human energy,
my splendid castle built of sand on sand.
Then tides do turn, and green-foamed surf moves in
to level it and wash it all away.
I watch my efforts crumble yet again.
Perhaps another beach, another day.

When Winter Comes

When age
whispers ice-cold facts
of shrinking time and soon closed doors,
I must write
brave stories to warn the young how
brief their strength, for life is and
is not.

Who Knows?

for Dolories

Poor Callie stares, these days, at hollyhocks
aligned along the garden fence. She sees,
perhaps, small lady dolls in frilly frocks,
herself a child at play—to find heart's ease.
A year ago it was, her reckless son
was chased by cops for running one red light,
and, in the aftermath, oblivion
as flames and sirens overran the night.
Then late this March the blizzard closed the road,
so Tom, her husband, left his car to try
to make it home along the lane he'd mowed
last summer, and where now he'd, frozen, lie.
    Her world destroyed by fire and ice, who knows
    the raging pain beneath her white repose?

After Loss, the Climb

She climbs the winding stairs of crumbling stone,
the steps moss-slick and narrow, ancient, steep,
while, down below, the ever-present grief
broods long in lonely pools and shadows deep.

She won't go back to sorrow, but move on.
By toe-holds, she will make her way alone.
To find the sun-warmed country place called Peace,
she climbs the winding stairs of crumbling stone.

The Last of Language, Then, Is This

"In postmodernism, language is believed to be incapable of representing final truth or reality....The possibility of any final interpretation of language must be endlessly deferred."
David K. Naugle

The building blocks, the ABC's
of Life's spare language,
heap themselves in tumbled piles,
awaiting rearrangement.

This generation's child will throw
the blocks in rank confusion
until a teacher comes to place
her cool white hand upon the pulse,
instructing in seclusion.

With absolutes now passe',
the age's bawdy nights close old;
the wearied suns rise late, ringed gray
with languid disillusion.

Could programmed research lead to light,
faint letters might be traced
on mountain walls, in caverns dry,
to cry the ancient knowledge stored,
secured for such a day.

Instead, bland words are published
in opulent profusion:
dissembled truth—or disassembled—
with no whisper of conclusion.

Long-grieved children, fearing silence,
babble verse until they die.
The last of language, then, is this:
without interpretation
one drawn sigh.

Impervious

Your words
plop
against my faith
as water
drops on
stone.

Water
may even
hollow out
stone—
but not
for centuries.

Fire and the Knife

in remembrance of Elaine Middleton

Abraham, that brave old man,
took fire and his whetted knife
for the three-day journey
into loss.

If his hand trembled, we are not told.

We know only
that his faith roared
hot as any furnace
to consume his best-loved.

That day a lamb moved in the thicket
and blessed the gathering:
slack-mouthed servants, waiting afar;
Isaac bound;
and Abraham, the friend of God,
whose compliance leaves us
silent.

It did not end with deliverance.
There is always that next journey
into loss.

Moriah will have us all.

Bearing our best-loved thing,
we come by choice or circumstance,
our highest hope defenseless before
the fire, the knife.

No one knows until he comes there:
Will his hand tremble?
Will the thicket move?

I Have Seen a Bird Soar Suddenly

As one acquainted with pain's darkened rooms
where light is barred, shut out like some rude guest,
I know how hopes ring hollow as from tombs
and nights creak slowly, offering no rest.
I know the pallid calm that pain puts on
to greet the anxious faces in a day
already shattered by the weight of dawn,
that seems, despite its sunrise, leaden gray.
But I have seen a bird soar suddenly,
then heard his song as fresh as running streams,
and so it is when I am loosed, set free
to write my songs and wing beyond dark themes.
  I watch for this though joy be now deferred,
  for pain will never have the final word.

The God of All Comfort

"A beggar's cup outstretched,
the world cries in its sleep."

I speak to you who knows despair,
Who longs to find a faithful friend,
I promise there is one who'll care.

He has concern for how you fare,
Your deepest needs he'll comprehend.
I speak to you who knows despair.

Encouragement, these days, is rare,
Of course, you doubt. I'll not pretend;
I promise, still, one who will care.

You want someone who'll help you bear
The heaviness that makes you bend,
That holds you in this long despair.

So take the challenge. Why not dare
Believe and let your prayer ascend?
The one who knows your heart will care.

The Comforter comes to prepare
All that you need—a true Godsend.
To you who bore this great despair,
Now taste His love, receive His care.

IV

In the Morning of the World

"Our lives were so thronged with small beauties, it was as though we were children of the rainbow, dwelling always in the morning of the world."

Bryan MacMahon,
Children of the Rainbow

In the Garden

Long ago I played in a backyard where flat stones were placed to form a stairway in the grass. It was just three steps down to what I called the Magic Garden. There, pink roses spilled over the white board fence. The mint grew thick in that sheltered corner, while, in the progressive dazzle of summer, cherries dotted one tree, peaches drooped among the branches of another, and sweet grapes scented the arbor. A large, mossy stone, put there, who knows when, became a royal throne or anything my imagination could conceive. On a hot day, I would pump water from the deep well, take a drink, and press my face against the cool concrete of the shaded well platform. It was the morning of the world.

The Well Room

Our iceman strides through the kitchen,
gripping the tongs that grip the ice
that goes in the well room.

All is coolness there,
the ice box with its ice blocks,
the damp chill from the cellar door.
In season, the sweet odors of the grape arbor
drift in. The peach trees, the whisper of vines,
keep the well room dimly green in summer.

It is an orderly place of jars and crocks—
tomato juice, bread and butter pickles,
strawberry preserves—a place to skim milk
and store the cream.

Flowers are arranged in the well room,
drooping armloads of lilac on the old oak table,
with stiff-stemmed gladioli, pink roses, white peonies,
or bright cosmos and a rainbow of zinnias
to fill the vases and wicker baskets.

Radishes are scrubbed in the clear well water,
and leaf lettuce, spring green.
By August, strings of peppers hang on the south wall.
Golden apples, a bushel at a time, have their corner
in autumn. In the sharp cold of winter, ropes
of taffy and homemade fudge await a party.
On Christmas Eve, rich custard cools in the well room,
with a walnut cake, well-aged.

Impossible to imagine the time when
this will be a junk room for broken chairs,
when no one will know its rightful name.

The Trunk Room

Visualize a small upstairs room, high-ceilinged,
with one tall narrow window looking to the sunset.
Imagine evening skies of fiery gold or grim crimson,
flaming orange or somber rose,
darkening to purple.

Remember, this is a room that belongs to the day.
Picture, at sundown, how it begins to turn in on itself,
how the trunks ranged in rows along the walls
seem strangely different in the shadows. Know that
the trunk room is a place where children play,
but never after dark.

Understand that by day the trunks are jolly old things
to climb on, chubby containers of odd leftovers
from lives lived in the dusty past. Suspect that at night
the ghosts rise from them to have their say.
Realize that family history does have its ghosts.
Leave them to their ancient sorrows
when darkness comes.

Hush, My Child

A screech owl screams in the night.
Good children, fooled by the implication
of terror, doom, and desolation,
huddle together, then cry for the light,

for Mother to restore their tilted world.

Her tenderness overcomes fretting and fright
as, cuddled, they hear her explanation
and learn by gentle illustration
what brings humanity through the night,

how Love with its comforts swallows up fear:
"Hush, My child, the Truth is here."

Waiting Out the Storm

Our family sleeps upstairs
in the tall white house
on the highest hill of Frankford.

On summer nights
when the wind rises
and thunder shakes the world,
we come downstairs to wait it out.

I pad down with the grownups,
my feet bare below my little girl nightgown,
white and soft from many washings,
and I curl into the couch.

I am both asleep and awake, floating,
sensing power in blast, crash, boom
deeper and bigger than the world—
like God's voice, I think.

The lights go out!
In the darkness lightning
cracks open the air,
all of us lit up for a second,
then dark again.

Finally, the low growl
of thunder moving away. . . .
"It's over," someone says.

The sweet, cool freshness
of a clean world comes in
through the open door.

For a lifetime I remember that great calm
when the winds cease—
the refreshment of God's Afterward.

These silvery clouds
hang between me and the moon.
Oh—it's lopsided!

Paradelle of the Stairs

When I was small, the stairs of our family home connected two worlds–Down where adults worked and Up where I played. The stairway, which seemed to me impossibly high and light-filled, was my enchanted world between. This paradelle expresses the mystique of those stairs where I found my separate identity.

The Paradelle is a French fixed form of six-line stanzas. In the first three stanzas, the second and fourth lines repeat the first and third lines. The fifth and sixth lines must use all the words from the preceding lines, but only those words. The last stanza must use every word from all the preceding stanzas, but only those words.

To the child, a stairway is a separate world,
To the child, a stairway is a separate world
And like uphill terrain one must cross,
And like uphill terrain one must cross.
A child must cross uphill to the world,
And, like a stairway, one is separate terrain

When you reach for what lies between the living room,
When you reach for what lies between the living room
And regions of the smiling moon, you find stairs,
And regions of the smiling moon, you find stairs.
You reach for the moon, find regions of room, and
the smiling, living lies when, between you, what stairs!

There, in truth, we need each higher step on the way,
There, in truth, we need each higher step on the way,
Where upstairs becomes our private, sacred place,
Where upstairs becomes our private, sacred place.
We place each step in private on the way upstairs,
There where sacred truth becomes our higher need.

On the stairway, a smiling child must step uphill.
Like the moon, one becomes a living place between.
There, where you need higher regions of world,
You reach for room, and find what and when.
The way to upstairs lies in each private truth.
We cross our separate stairs; the terrain is sacred.

The Playhouse

We drank cold tea
in our green willow tent,
the earth smelled smoky

and sweet and wild,
ate ripe apricots
spilt from a tree,

savored the juice
still on our lips,
child and child,

played house and planned
the white lace day when,
twenty-one, we'd find

the great-laid walls
of the grown-up world
now hid from our minds,

let cool willow limbs
brush our china doll
faces, so young

we didn't know about
hot desert places and
a white lace summer

without pity—roof of tin,
could not know in our
dim green world of then.

My Deliverer

for my father, Guy Chalmer Okes

It was Zella Mae's idea. "Let's go out there and sit," she said. "We can pretend we're on the edge of a cliff, looking down into a valley, a looooong way down. Won't that be fun?" "Ahuh," I said. I was a scaredy cat, but I didn't want her to know it. I followed her lead, climbing over the tall banister in the upstairs hall and stepping out onto a narrow shelf, built above the open stairwell for ornamentation. Usually, it held an oriental vase of dried grasses. Would it hold up two chunky kids? My mouth dust-dry, I awkwardly plopped down next to Zella Mae, with our legs dangling over ten feet of empty air. As she giggled and wriggled, the shelf creaked. My stomach felt hollow and my head whirled when I looked down and thought about where I was. Just then Daddy appeared below, coming up the stairs, his back to the wall where we were suspended. He had reached the top of the stairs before he realized we were perched on the shelf. His face froze into surprise, and I saw our danger in his eyes. "Give me your hand, Glory," he said in a voice that didn't sound like his. I reached toward rescue. The next moment he had lifted me up and over the banister to safety, then my playmate. She thought we were in trouble, but he didn't fuss at me, not at all. My father knew by the way I held on to him that I had learned that particular lesson. This was not the first time Dad had delivered me out of difficulty, nor would it be the last.

A Water-Baby's Summer

at my grandparents' farm where a little brown book
from Mommie Hanson's bookcase aroused my interest
in poetry, nature, and all things mystical.

I swam in dew the summer I was eight,
a water-baby in a sea of green,
where pastures lapped against the golden sheen
of morning rising at the eastern gate,
and I, I tasted beauty for that hour,
thirsty as a bee before a single flower.

"Please wake me up," I'd beg the busy farm,
afraid of missing some delicious sight,
or scent, or sound, or touch of airy light.
At five a.m. a hand would pat my arm.
Though hard asleep when called, I could not wait
to swim in joy that summer I was eight.

While others rose to work, I rose to play.
I petted woolly lambs, explored the creek;
among some ancient tree roots, gnarled, unique,
I made a house for all my dolls one day.
But domesticity was not my mien,
this water-baby in a sea of green.

I wandered far as my young feet could go,
I rode bareback on Rex—as free as air,
I felt that I could follow any dare
and make my choice without an adult's No.
My independence gained, a valued trait,
I loved my life the summer I was eight.

(cont.)

And when I dipped into the room of books,
I found a tale so magical and wise,
I read and read with fascinated eyes,
well-hidden in my secret outdoor nooks
with my new friend, the author, C. Kingsley,
and *Water-Babies* dwelling in the sea.

Now fifty years beyond, I look again
at that small book, an heirloom I keep still,
remembering a dawn-fresh, dew-soaked hill,
returning to that golden summer when
I fell in love with truth in poetry,
a water-baby in an endless sea.

Summer, 1941

We pull ourselves through the long grass,
spying on Nazis while the grownups
sit on the front porch and speak of war.

Swallows circle and dive on their way to the barn.
With enemy aircraft overhead we freeze,
don't move a muscle.

The sun goes down.
Our pulses pound along with the night noises,
the katydids, the frogs at the pond.

Porch rockers creak, the trees hum.
The moon moves in and out of clouds.
We slither and crawl and run through the shadows.

Dangerously close, we crouch
at the corner of the house, alert to the flare
of a match, the pinpoint light of a cigarette tip.

If the Gestapo find us, we will die.
Fear and courage feel the same
in the sultry dark.

The grownups talk of war in Europe.
We live it out, our hearts as hot
as the Missouri summer.

The Pear Grove

Our life once seemed a storybook. It was when
the pear grove in our neighborhood took on
the lavish shape and furnishings
of some fabled outdoor room, richly carpeted,
with aisles of velvet grass and leafy roof
against the pale blue porcelain of sky.
There we treaded lightly in the hush
of sumptuous shade. Those pears, still green, dangled
within our reach, so we plucked and ate the fruit,
tart, yet faintly sweet, crunchy as a piece of ice.

This feast could be observed by Mrs. Cash
behind the curtain, her waxy fingers
moving net aside to beckon, "Children, come."
She was the friendly witch of the bay-windowed
house where the dense array of pear trees gloomed
her lofty, cluttered maze of shadowed rooms.
Like children in a fairy tale, we'd walk
into that house, enchanted place of dust
unchecked, of seashells, ancient toys, cascade
of books and mountainous piles of magazines.

No one told us she was a sad recluse
and so we visited the way we took
our ease within the pear grove, living out
the magic with a love for the strange.
We dwelt inside the Story—were the Story—
that green and shaded summer we were ten.

Intrusion in the Grass

Skimming March winds
across our pasture,
I stop at the well
which has no pump,
old, abandoned, boarded,
a mystery among the cattle.

Why there
in the middle of bare field?
Who dug it, discarded it
long before we came?
What hides beneath
its rude cover?

I kite-fly,
dodge the bull,
spin stories about that
out-of-place, odd, of-no-use well.
I cross by on my way to play
and wonder.

But when Granny dies
my dog and I
head for a place apart—
the well
marked with rough-piled rock
in the autumn stubble.

(cont.)

I refuge by it,
arms clutching
friendly fur.
My dog waits
while I weep
and learn the taste of loss.

I never go back to the well again.
I suppose it still *is*—
an intrusion in the grass,
like grief and graves
and death.

Guided Tour

There where the wall ends at the corner,
behind the white lilac bush, fat with leaves
and blossoms, I used to hide myself from view,
dangling my legs over the wall, surveying
the old road on its way to the pond,
its alluring brambles and Queen Anne's Lace.

Back here in the grape arbor on warm afternoons
I played paper dolls, or took my book
under the damson plum tree in the orchard
where the grass felt like cool silk to bare feet
and I could snack on the fruit as I read.

Come September, I had to walk down that hill
to the red brick school house where strident
teacher voices ruled the world, where the bell
clanged at recess end, and thirsty, sweaty,
jostling children waited in line to march inside.

I still remember the delights of orchard and wall,
the way I felt, the thoughts I dreamed there.
Of school, I only recall the way we endured,
like beasts of the field in bad weather,
apparently thinking nothing at all.

Unclassified

I went to School
But was not wiser
Emily Dickinson

I am a child. I draw
only sticks of men, box houses
unclassified,
and those absurd girl faces
with swollen cheeks and staring
doll-dull eyes.

My fingers
cannot translate
complexities; instead,
blobbed colors
of the school-desk day:
purples with grass green globes
and orange-reds leaning
into lines, margins
defaced.

The subtleties of shape,
defined
and separate,
are for cunning, artful hands
that, drawing, somehow see—
and, seeing, understand.

A Memory

In the last year of World War II,
Peveley Dairy used horses to deliver milk in St. Louis.
Trapped near an open window, I could hear
their peaceful hoofs clip-clopping
                                        down Union Avenue.

Inside our classroom, Melba was trying to read
the first page of *Legend of Sleepy Hollow.*
The words were coming out painfully, separately,
like individual teeth being extracted
                                        without an anesthetic.

Melba could not read, but she could weep. There was
no escaping her shame, her red, tear-streaked face,
and Miss Klay's bullying, punishing voice, demanding
what Melba could not give,
                                        grating on our soul.

And the horses' peaceful hoofs clip-clopped
                                        down Union Avenue.

Peonies

One spring when I was seven,
I wrote on peony leaves,
    marking the underside where
fine-ribbed veins made divisions on the severed leaf,
compartments I could measure with my thumb
while I puzzled out my world.

When the peonies bloomed that May,
my short legs cleared the tallest bush
    without touching a single giant blossom.
Petals heavy with fragrance nodded in the breeze
while I shouted in triumph.

On Memorial Day the peonies looked stiff
and solemn, their globes of pink and white
    propped in wicker baskets
for our people in their graves.
I placed a single flower for Gertrude, ten years old,
who had died of typhoid fever in 1896.

That's how it was then:
the shout of life, the silence of death
    in separate compartments,
yet mingled with those great, sweet peonies.

Now I write on recycled paper,
reconciling life and death
    through the Resurrection.
Though peonies bloom in the brief, cold spring,
then fade, we can forever sing:
"He lives! He lives! Christ Jesus lives today!"

Summer Place

I spent the best parts of 30 summers at our Okes family home. I thought it was the most beautiful house in the world, and the happiest way to live. I have never found another memory to equal the ordered peace and grace of that place.

A fruit basket sunset of peach and plum,
the scent of lemon lilies in the air.
Swallows are circling home to their nests,
while cicadas sing in the locust trees.

I ramble at dusk in a field of fireflies,
keep company with the evening star.
Later, wrapped in the dreamy dark,
I rest content in an Adirondack chair.

I sleep upstairs by an open door where
the Chinese elms weave shadow patterns
of moonlight and leaf. Sounds of life
from woods and pond drift in with the breeze.

Ever after, I measure my times
by the memorable summers at Frankford.
Shaped by those gentle seasons, I find
my summer place is now a state of mind, of grace.

I Sing of Sword-Bright Love

for my mother, Irene Hanson Okes

Weaving a song
For Mother's ear,
I find most dear
These shining ways:

Your steely love
That steadfast stays
Through dulling days
Intensely bright,

Your standing strong,
Prepared to fight
For daughter's right
To be, and do.

Such loyalty
Deserved by few
Comes free from you,
For I belong.

V

Young on the Shore

"In the breaking dawn of eternity we shall discover that God could not have brought us by another route which would have been as expeditious or as safe as the one by which we have come."

F. B. Meyer,
The Shepherd Psalm

Young on the Shore

Cornucopia, Wisconsin

We were young on the shore
of Lake Superior

We measured rough
waves the hard blue
of sapphire
lightly counted ship
carcasses rotting under
a severe sky

We tramped the empty beach
challenged a storm-born
wind until chilled
we ceded driftwood and
retreated still laughing

Undaunted, we searched across
desert reaches of open water
believed we'd find a lighthouse
somewhere

We were young (and wise)
on the shore

Snapshot

for Keith and Michael

We are on our way to Lake Geneva,
the road narrow, the day warm,
with no air conditioning in 1960.

The traffic moves like a ponderous snake.
Dan sees some room ahead and speeds up.
We are near a Wisconsin town,
and the local sheriff stops us.

The boys in the back seat squirm.
They are too young to be awed
by civic authority, but not
too young to feel hot and cross.

Dan silently hands over his license.
The man with the badge peers
into our English Ford station wagon
and sees the two small boys,
their heads blond as the sun,
their eyes blue as the lakes.

He chuckles! "I'm going to fine you,"
he tells Dan in high good humor.
"I sentence you to buy ice cream cones
for these fine young men. Just stop
at that drive-in down the road there."

Lake Geneva sparkles in the sun
like a painting of white sails on royal blue water.
Our boys' eyes shine. "Look!" they shout,
pointing with delight at a red sailboat,
their fair hair ruffling in the wind.

In my mind I take a snapshot
of this moment to enjoy
forty years later.

About My Husband

"So ought men to love their wives
as their own bodies. He that loveth
his wife loveth himself."
Ephesians 5:28

Father in Heaven,
who designed husbands
to love their wives
the way Christ loved
his church,

I thank you for my husband.
Before, I feared I'd clutch and cling
and thought I should stand alone
with our arms touching,
but still alone, individually braced.

Now I know he is mine to rest upon
even as we both rest upon you.
Every gift you give is good;
how then could I have misunderstood
your plan for marriage?

I thank you for my husband,
who cherishes his wife,
who, for love of me, would give his all,
even give his life, and in response I honor him.
Like Sarah, I freely call him lord!

With Dan
On Grey Rock Trail

Poudre Canyon, Colorado

Our tawny dog crossed
the footbridge first,
glad to be running free.
Winter had loosed its hold,
but we still could see
snow clinging to the pines
and feel it damp and sobering
when it plopped on the face.
To compensate, the moss
on the boulders grew
bright spring-green.

Up on the trail
we found
a small stream
bubbling down
to the Poudre River,
and, in a green-arched hall
of pines, we sat on a flat rock
and talked,
then stood together,
our cheeks touching for warmth
while we prayed.

Blackberries

at Delightsome Land

Three things I like
about picking blackberries:

The astonishing beauty
of the berries on the bush—
poetic shapes, luscious colors,

The cool of our spring
and the taste of the water
after a hot hour's work,

The walk home
across the pasture with you.

Marriage by Moonlight

Anniversary Song

The world lies all translucent in the night;
the white moon gleams, an upturned silver bowl,
spilling its shine to bathe these two in light,
their faces softly touched by aureole
of radiance, their beings merged, made whole.
The lovers glory in this joy on loan
from Heaven where all happiness is sown.

From Heaven where all happiness is sown
these two explore the treasure house of Time;
with lavish, heaped-up years to call their own,
they learn to live as one in fluid rhyme
and move to private music, chime by chime.
The valued vow of constancy they keep,
sealed even as they turn to touch in sleep.

Sealed even as they turn to touch in sleep,
they slip from moonlit youth to star-drawn age
and dream their life again—now time to reap
the full-grown harvest of their heritage
and taste the tenderness of this last stage.
While lovers wait their journey into Light,
the world lies all translucent in the night.

To Hear That Song

To love
may yet mean to grieve,
to feel the steely thrust of loss,
for I know
life is as brief as one bird's song,
but to hear that song, I'll pay
the price.

Siamese Dreaming

My cat is contemplative.
She lazes in pools of thought,
her blue Siamese eyes dreaming
of ancient temples, fountains tinkling
in courtyards where the ages pause.

Stretching with sinuous grace
she recalls regal prowls
in jungles past
where prey met claws
springing out of the green
cascades of steaming forest.

Tranquil, she smoothes her creamy fur
and regards her padded paws
while awaiting milky poured libation.
Pondering the worship due her,
she accepts my daily adoration.

Last Call

I call
my proud Black Lab
(now old and almost blind).
"Prince! Prince Caspian!"
A hoot owl dourly answers.
Clutching a light,
I cross darkening fields,
peer into mists, stumble
to the spring where Prince
once splashed and drank.
Out of the deep woods
where Tarzan vines hang thick
on towering trees,
I think I hear his bark.

I wait . . . hope . . . plunge into the dark.

As I walk slowly back
across the pasture
now alive
with tiny firefly lights,
I smell crushed grapes,
too ripe,
fallen to the ground.
I wonder,
did Prince choose the forest
where once he ran as mighty hunter?
Grapes must over-ripen in due time.
Dogs must age and die.
But I cry.

At the Edge of Morning

"His mercies never come to an end;
they are new every morning."
Lamentations 3:23 RSV

All
done, now
cock's crow tolls
the death of
night, in the same
spent breath
salutes this
Dawn.

Awake
from the pit of
sleep—entangled by
warm sheets, pillowed
deep—I
face the open
space of
Day.

Who
knows the circus
whirl of time bent
so, the dizzying
turn of streets I'll
meet, perhaps
traverse? Only
God.

The Way Light Comes

The way the sunlight
strikes my right
eye unexpectedly
reminds me how Light
comes.

This light has pierced
through closures,
finding its path between
mini-blinds
duly shut against
the new day.

It is urgent,
inconvenient,
stabbing me
into acknowledgement
of its presence.
I cannot ignore it
until a more convenient time.

In the computer screen
I see my face reflected,
the curve of my cheek
striped with light
and shadow.

House of Snow

a Rondeau

A house of snow, this seems to me.
Encased in pleasant lethargy,
I doze and dream, but do not go
where dreams would take me on tiptoe,
confronting new geography.

For hungry birds, a sympathy;
surrounded by my books and tea,
protected from the winds that blow—
a house of snow.

If sun should offer liberty,
quick-thawing with a remedy
for one still caught in embryo,
no doubt I'd stay with what I know:
this winter-wrapped security—
a house of snow.

Going On

A coyote crossed our upper pasture,
        alone and purposeful.

His gaunt silhouette moving against
        the grayish rose of early morning

told me life was going on
        even when I said, Stop.

To the LORD of Gates and Doors

The Roman god of gates and doors
with two faces looking in opposite directions
presided at the beginning of the year
and my birth, mythology says.
From Janus, then, my affinity with time,
my fascination with gates
and open doors?

Does this also picture my perilous place
between two opposing forces?
Prodded from within,
pressed from without,
persuaded, pushed, pulled about,
put up, put down, put out . . .
Please!

O True God of gates and doors
that open wide upon Your Word,
O LORD of Time and times
that perform all the counsel of Your will,
O King of Kings and Prince of Peace,
teach me how to walk the balance beam.
Reconcile me with myself.

Spring Rain
At Murphy Park

The park lies green and empty under rain.
Unruffled ducks glide along the empty banks.
Raindrops pattern their watery path.

Two geese take their gosling
to the island at the center of the lake.
A lilac dusk descends upon the silence.

It needs this leisure, our park, so often strained
with children's shouts, wheels turning,
walkers and runners churning the air.

I sit at a damp picnic table
to soak in the silence.
People, like parks, require renewal.

The clouds pass, and stars appear.
There is a creamy moon. As a child, I fancied
I could trace a caring man's face on its surface.

Tonight I look beyond to the Maker of lights,
to the One who has cared for me.
All I have needed has been provided.

He will come to us
as the spring rains that water the earth.

From One Who Has Not World Enough, and Time

"But at my back I always hear
Time's wingèd chariot hurrying near."
Andrew Marvell

The daring of birds
who bring sun-spilled lawns
to life
is just beginning.
This season of birds
and blue ageratum and zinnias that blaze
along the garden wall
seems as sure as the sundial's
moving shadow.

But here with the whole host
of favored months spread before my eyes
like vistas seen from Mt. Pisgah,
I look to November,
to the dread of winter,
for I cross my bridges
early
and summer begins its arcing descent
with the bright-splintered fall
of the last Roman
candle.

Renewal
At The Cedars

for Cousin Hazel,
Huntsville, Alabama

Here, I am coddled by old things—
ancient cedars, hickory, oaks,
aged stone seats amid the vinca,
the venerable boxwood hedge
bordering a long walk,
the weathered white-washed brick,
the great stone chimneys,
the Georgian facade facing south . . .

The Cedars, built in 1818, knows how to shelter.
I feel secure, at peace, behind these walls,
as though strong people had invested
their own virtue in the house and garden.
Their living history flows about me.

The sweet purple phlox and four o'clocks
bloom on freshly as though they have always
been. Only the birds seem young,
and suddenly I am young again,
a happy child, picking ripe figs
and white ginger lilies for the supper table.

Renewal begins this way—when we are
without expectation, when we come
to a tall closed gate of ornamental iron,
and it opens to us.
It opens!

In Praise of Age
And One Green Leaf

I celebrate one perfect leaf
that swings ripe-green against the sky,
fern-green on blue as freshly blue
as northern lakes in stirring air
where mirrored pines and sun-shot ripples
waver in the wind.
                                        Those splendid winds
from other days now send their sounds
through Time and times to where,
in this more cloistered year, I hear
the clear-toned bells of peace
and pause to praise one perfect leaf.

"Making Melody in My Heart"

After *Ephesians 5:19*

Blue as the pool that mirrors the sky,
green as the ferns that grow nearby . . .
sweet as the wild rose that rambles the ground,
clean as the rain with its lyrical sound . . .
fragrant as lilac and mint by the well,
clear as the meadow lark's morning swell . . .
free as the wind that sends forth the breeze,
great as the spreading giant oak trees . . .
high as the heavens, warm as the sun,
gentle as twilight when the day's done . . .
fair as the stars that sparkle by night,
peaceful as pastures under moonlight . . .
fresh as the dawn, exquisite as dew
when day breaks and mercies come to me new—
Earth, you are beauty! To Christ be all praise,
Creator and Author of glorious days,
Who gives joy by the moment, hope for the end,
my Savior and Sovereign, my Unchanging Friend.

Nesting

Give me the flamy comfort
of Bach organ works
to redden the pale day,

Old solidity
of the wood stove
to warm my winter self,

Sounding chimes
of the Seth Thomas clock
to count a country peace . . .

Five p.m., day's end,
time to shut out
the November spread of dark.

Beyond my shuttered window
snowbirds stir the bushes,
nesting for night

like me, in their small serenity.

Wintering
In Northwest Arkansas

A great simplicity has come.
Blackberries from the thorny hill
float in white milk. The stain spreads,
          and the sweetness.

Quiet words enfold the hour.
A homemade fire shawls our shoulders.
The kitten mews for loving,
          purrs, satisfied.

Outdoors, the fading sun
spills pale as cream across
the japonicas where small birds
          are sheltering.

Fires may die and kittens cry forlorn.
A low white sky tomorrow
may mean sleet or drifting snow.
          Anything may happen.

But great simplicity has come.

Red December On Flint Creek

Stubble blushes
with rosy glow
where grass once stirred,

Shaggy cattle
sport winter coats
bright auburn-furred,

Cardinals wing
past coppery bridge
to snowy nest,

Sundown trumpets
late crimson light
from clouding west.

Month of embers:
cloaked December's
red-hued Winterfest.

To Taste the Years

The spice of candles, cookies,
piney wreaths and wassail
scents my Christmas dreams.

And could I greedy childlike
chase through time
running back I would find
that mystic hall
where memories are stored,
as honeyed, pungent, rainbowed,
tingling, chuckling, firelight-warming
as before when they were all.

I would dip into each cupboard
to taste the years and sample
my delicious past.

This Ending

I watch the old year drifting down,
dull-dappled green, rose-bronze, barred-brown,
falling gently like a leaf,
fading simply without grief.

A time of old gold, ragged tawn,
these drying hours we tread upon,
like dying leaves in the grass,
crumpled under as we pass.

I see the old year paling gray,
diminished, clouding, mauve-mood day
swept by shifting, somber breeze,
thinly marked by spare-limbed trees.

The time of aging, time of change,
looms certain as a mountain range
now in view and very near,
this quiet ending of a year.

Curtain Call

My window on the night
    Presents a few
    Fine stars in view,
The clouds like drifts of snow,
The moon a silver kite,
    Unmoored and high
    In winter's sky—
Till gray dawn ends the show.

On the Long Drive North

I see the river charged with chunks of ice,
a pond metallic in the freezing mist,
one gaunt white house with darkened hulk of barn,
and stand of bluish spruce that separates
the wide white fields from strangely-whitened sky.
All this I see before new snow comes down
to slant across the road like curtains drawn
against the night, and we must drive on north.

"A tumultuous privacy of storm,"
one poet said of old-time snows that shut
whole families within their stout-built walls
to celebrate the rituals of clan,
communal life around the cozy hearth.
They stayed at home in staunch togetherness,
while we must trek three hundred miles to find
the place where briefly we can share our loss.

Our sturdy van plows on into the storm,
as, silently, deep hollows fill with snow.
In lieu of fireside, we have dashboard lights,
the heater keeps on blasting blown-air warmth,
and we rely on trusted comradeship,
I with him, he with me, no matter what.
We face our brother's death, this winter gale,
as we have always lived, by faith and love.

(cont.)

Long windshield wipers sweep across the glass,
headlights delineate a narrow path.
Our vision checked by sleet and snow and dusk,
we strain to see. Our eyes would probe ahead.
How many times we've tried to search the dark,
to know how we should go, to test ourselves
on what's beyond and prove that we are fit.
Yet wisdom teaches us to wait for grace.

And grace is what we need to ride these years
when north winds mourn and ice encrusts the road.
We smile at one another and reach out
to touch before we pray for travelers,
offering thanks that in such storms as these,
God blankets us with care, gives all we need.
There, up ahead, a loving welcome waits . . .
Light through opened doors, shining on the snow.

About the Poems

As a teacher and poetry critic, Gloria Okes Perkins encourages younger poets to find their voice. Desiring to make this book useful for those who are working to develop their craft and master new forms, she has requested that a complete list of the poetry forms and rhyming patterns from *After Eden*, be included in the appendix, with page numbers for reference.

Most of the poems of this collection have been prized and/or published in Christian magazines, anthologies, newspaper columns, and poetry journals such as *Voices International, The Sand Cutter, The Inkling, Rockford Review, Pegasus, Tradition, Christian Poetry Journal, Stepping Stones, Berries from the Thorny Hill,* and *Prize Poems of the NFSPS.* Awards include the Grand Prize of the Poetry Society of Arizona, the Edgar Allan Poe Memorial Award of the Poetry Society of Virginia, the Poet Laureate Award from Poets Roundtable of Arkansas, the Grace Vantwerp Woodward Award from the National Federation of State Poetry Societies, and many more.

Poetry Forms and Rhyming Patterns

Free Verse

Richard and Janis Shull are award-winning nature and wildlife photographers from Mena, Arkansas, in the heart of the beautiful Ouachita Mountains. They live outside the city on 40 wooded acres with a small pond where Janis maintains her family of feathered pets—ducks, geese, and guineas—plus three sugar gliders (Australian marsupials resembling flying squirrels). The Shulls' work, including aerial photography, has appeared in publications, on billboards, in private collections, and regional shows. They also teach photography classes and coordinate the annual photography show sponsored by Mena Art Gallery. Prior to their move to Mena, Richard was a budget officer for the University of Arkansas, and Janis was a nurse educator in the field of mental health.

Mary Alice Larson is an essayist, playwright, and poet, but she considers teaching her special calling. She taught English composition and literature at Central Missouri State and Southwest Missouri State colleges and has been an elementary school teacher in Missouri and Florida. An expert in children's literature and a popular story teller, she worked for eight years in the Children's Department of the Rogers, Arkansas, Public Library where she had opportunity to indulge in her chief delight: creating and directing skits and plays, often with audience participation. Although she has enjoyed residence in Key West, Florida, and Santa Fe, New Mexico, her heart is rooted deep in the forested hills of the Ozarks. She presently resides in Springdale, Arkansas.

Pamela Solakian is a renowned watercolorist with studios in Ventura County, California. Her paintings, which have gained numerous awards, can be found in private and corporate collections in the United States and abroad. Well-known for her rose art and featured in *Romantic Homes,* she was commissioned to paint the official rose of England's Princess Diana. The transparency and freshness in her watercolors is beautifully portrayed in nature close-ups, garden scenes, and skyscapes. Pamela's keen eye and love of nature has inspired her creativity since early childhood. She writes, "I feel a tremendous sense of joy when I capture nature's soft intricate beauty in watercolor and am able to share this with others."

LaVergne, TN USA
16 July 2010
189765LV00003B/3/P